Earth Touch

An Anthology

To my friend
Derma

From your sister in Christ,

Valerie

Philippians 3:13-14
9-17-2023

Visit www.booksurge.com to order additional copies.

Earth Touch

An Anthology

VJ Chapman

Dedication

Dedicated to my Lord and Savior, Jesus Christ

Acknowledgements

A special thanks to those whose endless courage, love, creativity, and encouragement are a constant source of inspiration:

My soul mate, Lucas
Parents, Robert and Naomi McGarry
Sister, Vanessa P. Dalton
Granddaughter, Nicole L. Bergen
Pastor Leland Keithley
Pastor Joel Osteen

In Loving Memory of:

Grandfather, Homer Toedtemeier
Parents, Luke and Chloie Chapman
Mother, Jean Dousett O'Brien
Uncle, Donald McGarry
Brother, Edgar McGarry
Son, Gabriel Mark Chapman
Daughter, Naomi Eve Chapman

And in appreciation to:

Our children, Gabriel, Naomi, Elisabeth, Luke, and
    Matthew Chapman
The Chapman Family
The McGarry Family
Uncle Doug Dousett
Dear friends, Marjorie Cavins, Nini Starr, Jodi DeTal,
    Clare Predeek, Lorinda Bergen
Teacher, Carol Bridgens
Publishing Consultant, David Beckmann
Editorial Coordinator, Sandy Shalton
Editor, Joanne S.
Account Management Team, Whitney, Lauren, Jack
Ben Thomas, Yes Graphics

Introduction

"Thus saith the Lord: The heaven is my throne, and the earth is my footstool. Where is the house that ye build unto me? And where is the place of my rest? For all those things hath mine hand made, and all those things have been, saith the Lord; but to this man will I look, even to him that is poor and of a contrite spirit, and trembleth at my word."

Job 66:1–2 KJV

Table of Contents

I – Sonnets

"And now abideth faith, hope, love, these
three; but the greatest of these is love. "

I Corinthians 13:13 KJV

Morning Sonnet

The silver curtain rises once again;
A morning drama dawning in the east.
With spires aglow like faithful priestly men
Whose march began anew when darkness
    ceased,
They promptly echo onto whitened stage;
Illuminating waiting watching drops
Of dew-communion offered age to age.
Who will the sower find among the crops?
As peals of color split the silent sky,
Where deaf'ning swollen rainbows kneel to
    pray,
Then heaven opens up its golden eye;
A hush of quiet homage to the day.
The reaper finds reward who sleeps no more;
Awaken now before the dawn is o'er!

Infinity

Soon flying in on heaven's moistened wing,
With talons clutched in winter's mortal back,
Erupting in arrival thunder-crack,
To bowing tides and blessing clouds who bring
Their sun and moon and star-gem fitted ring.
Now christened marks the vigilant attack
Down sentenced earth's most futile trodden
    track,
Where e'en the purest eagles fail to cling.
In searching, seize the weight that bears a
    smile;
Who heals all wounds with signature
    unclaimed,
Devour all beauty's wine of mystery,
And screech redemption's carol all the while.
Then breathe a wrinkled parting unashamed,
And waft away in immortality.

Gift

There is a secret bolt about to blaze
That no one who was ever born could dream
Would burst upon a desert to redeem
The thirsty night, the barren mournful days.
A secret streak of thunder-laden praise
So soon to shake the rocks from what they
    seem
And soon to bring a pure celestial gleam
Song's last farewell to sin's forgotten days.
Yet shepherds knew and cattle met the dawn
When skies exclaimed with angels' interlace
The Glory of a bantam potent knight
Proclaiming winter's twilight time is gone
Silent sigh from heaven's hidden face
Reflected in the souls of yesternight.

Throes

The throes of our survival loom ahead
A rescue-shrouded economic slump
Debris descends and raging prices jump
From governmental socialistic dread
An agonizing hail of vows misled.
While thundered silence reads you for a chump
Don't be around to hear that mournful trump
Of angels seeking numbered hands and head.
Now reeling through the agony aghast
Now tumbling deep in poverty's crevasse.
Escape the earth's most agonizing pain
Before the Father sends a final blast
When hope is blind while seven corpses pass
And time's a vapor tethered to the mast.

II – Verse

"It is he who sitteth upon the circle of the earth, and the inhabitants thereof are like grasshoppers; who stretcheth out the heavens like a curtain, and spreadeth them out like a tent to dwell in: Who bringeth the princes to nothing; he maketh the judges of the earth as vanity."

Isaiah 40:22–23 KJV

Sunset

Who can give approval but a sunset
To all the toil and laughter of the day?
Shading all the dreary grays with crimson
And coaxing timid rainbows out to play.
Soft affirming music of a sunset
A final cymbal sounding out the smile
Finishing the scarlet-feathered journey
Of east to west philosophy and style.
Everyone's a dreamer in the sunset
Still whispering of mighty deeds undone
Holding on to mem'ries for tomorrow
Where hope for love and sunsets are begun.
Sunset, paint your promise in the heavens,
Let earth stretch out and heave a weary sigh,
Then wrap your faithful arms around the hours
Now spent in playful moments of good-bye.
Treetops yawn and wave a golden ending
To sadness and to joy that time has spun
Heads bow down in grateful admiration
Of the Maker who formed a setting sun

Answers

I know that the Lord always answers my
    prayers,
I know that He hears me; I know that He cares.
But sometimes His answer just isn't the one
On my mind when the asking begun.
At times it's an opposite notion from mine
Arriving far short of the scheduled design.
It seems that He's leaving my future to fate
When His answer is simply to wait.
Along comes a problem, a personal need;
Convinced I can solve it, I kneel down and
    plead
To God for permission to change things just so.
Then He tells me the answer is no.
And when I receive an occasional yes
It's always His answer for instant success.
Why, yes, you must finish the duty at hand
And He gives me the grace to withstand
The stubborn revolt rising up in my head
Procrastinate now, do it later instead.
They're not often verdicts of instant delight
But His answers will always be right.

Fallen Leaves

When autumn comes
On sure slow feet,
To tread over dreams
As stubbled wheat,
Then hopes once green
Are crushed and burned
In piles of defeat—
lifeless and spurned.
"A time to die"
Is in His plan
To renew with spring
The heart of man.
Will I mourn or praise
My autumn days?

Attendant

Comforting weary
Satisfied heart
Quenched by the circle of toil,
Bring me your emptied
Vessel of sway
Drawn by the sweltering soil.
Nodding, approving
Eyes fall and fail,
Caught by a bronze braided net;
Spirited dreamer
Left to explore,
Wrapped by desire's duet.
Angels above us
Piloting rest,
Rocked by the rhythm of tides
Brimming with quiet's
Fresh velvet milk
Nursed by a love that abides.

Vashti

She flies into hearts on butterfly wings with
    tenderness and beauty, fresh and new.
    Without predictability, she blossoms and
    changes saddened hearts to laughing ones.
From dull cocoons, all who are graced by her
    whispered flight burst forth into panoramic
    colors of moods and emotions, fleeting with
    joyful wings over paths of peacefulness.
And where she directs, eyes will say—I know
    this road, I've been this way. But over the
    last green mountain, there's an ocean never
    seen before…and no one has led you there.
    Her colors blend into a new brilliance,
    leaving always with a happy heart.

Betrothed

With compass-trust our vessel bears secure
Upon a jade abyss the master guides;
No depth or height could hush a course so
    pure,
But follow joy reflected in the tides.
A heart of love unconquered yet abides,
And though from breath my soul should ebb
    and flee,
I'll ever your endearing shadow be.

Disclosure

What do you see in the misty mirror
Of a whispering waterfall
In its elegant beckoning dances
Its quiet compassionate call?
Yesterday's sorrow may echo regret
Or visions of hope quench your soul
When you gaze in the crystalline curtain
The ivory bubbling bowl.
But the secret to what is reflected
Lies beneath the pearl-laden wall
Where the fingers of time etch the beauty
Of a mystical waterfall.

To Dance in Courage Circle

To dance in courage circle with her heart
To music never heard or rhythms sung.
For this she will with rusted trophies part,
And find the steps she used
When thoughts were young.
They were the rosy ones she danced among,
And his the leading stride that bade her start
To dance in courage circle with her heart
To music never heard or rhythms sung.
And you, the captured tune, so sweet thou art,
As lips of lilac singing songs unsung.
Brought end to end but never far apart,
Remaining here on raptured golden tongue
To dance in courage circle with her heart
To music never heard or rhythms sung.

Day's End

Let the moon be my pillow
I'm safe in his arms
Stars singing sweet lullabies
He covers me up—
A soft black blanket of night
With sleep, he closes my eyes.

The Climb

Standing at the foothill
Gazing up to lofty peak,
Eager for the journey
For the challenge that I seek.
High above the clamor
Looking upward to my goal,
Escaping in the climb
In a search to feed my soul.
Left behind the dulling gray
Embracing azure view
Exhilarating power
This mountain spirit new.
The giant yields release,
A conquering sigh of peace.

Edgar

Heaven's come between us now
Between your hand and ours;
How I pray I could somehow
Have God turn back the hours.
My heart is torn in anguish
As I lash out at pain;
A soul poured out lays languish
In sorrow's bitter rain.
You always brought me rainbows
And smiles to fill my eyes
And now I know that's why God chose
To let you leave without good-byes.

Smile

When your life hits a low
And there are troubles although
You've tried your best,

Nothing seems to go right
There's confusion despite
What they suggest;

Dig down in your heart
And find what is there.
It's easy to start
Attractive to wear.

Disturbances flee with cowardly style
At the sight of a genuine smile.

Duet

Walk with me along banks of
Green moisture and blue water,
Touch me with your laughter
And I'll not be afraid…

Speed across moons of silver sand
And meadows filled with red clover,
And I'll not be afraid…

Let me follow you always as a silent shadow
And let us together be as one;
Touch me with your love
And I'll not be afraid…

Because you'll be mine.

Sentinel

Greeter of mornings
Watcher of night
Arms touching wings
Of eagles in flight
Mighty in stature
Rooted in power
Beauty adorns
Earth's forest tower

Graduation

There are times in life though seldom
That a milestone comes along
Marking an accomplishment achieved,
And I'm standing in the spotlight
Yet reflecting on the past…
Thankful for the faithful who believed
That this day would always get here
And encouraged me and cheered,
"Finish; keep on running; never quit!"
I can almost hear their voices
And the prayers they must have breathed.
(No man is an island, I admit.)
Though at times I may have fallen,
I stood up to meet each foe;
Strengthened by the discipline of pain.
If I seemed quite overtaken
It was just a test of will
Prayers and faith have helped me to attain.
May I walk across the threshold
And begin a venture new—
Bold determination as my prize,
Then with humble recognition
Of how victories are won,
Hopes and dreams in others will arise.

Painted Spectrum Interlace

Crimson arc whose sins erase
Temple orange, cool embrace
Splash of amber woven lace
Ocean sea foam freshened face
Sapphire angel sorrows chase
Beryl cobalt auras trace
Far-reflected violet grace

If Not Tonight, Then Soon

If not tonight, then soon
Before the blood-red moon
Engulfs the souls of all of those
Who'd otherwise have flown
If not tonight then soon
Our winged flight enfold
Soon face-to-face
Soon arm-in-arm
We'll walk the streets of gold
If not tonight, then soon

Old Friend

Traces of yesterday's surviving
Now so useless
And foreign
Are discarded by the young.
But in the fire
There is a pain
The old cannot forget.
Tears seek a new escape
From the wounds of today.

Childhood

Was the laughter always so
Spontaneous and new?
Was the ease with which we ran
And jumped so simple too?
Not a care for small hearts
When the sun is out to play
Never gloom when raindrops
Or a snowflake greet the day.
Follow tiny footsteps
If it's heaven you would win,
For only those with childlike faith
Will ever enter in.

Weathered

When a storm-tossed heart
Has lost its way
Driven in waters
Troubled and gray
Then a ray of hope
Pierces the night
A matron shines
Her beacon light
With a heart set sail
For harbor's shore
Beams from her smile
Light the way before
Anchored in love
The lighthouse above

Celebration

May your day be filled with blossoms
Fresh with the dew of morn
May a "dream come true" bring fragrance
Petals your feet adorn

Through the Rain

I saw a bird alight in weather fair
The iridescent blue beset the sky
And coaxed the gentle breeze
To sway a tender bud and blossom there
Then from the ground a rumbling menace
    scorn
Did shake the wren and from its perch was
    shook
And onto earth a bounce
A rumbling shaking trounce
Away the sunny glistening song was squelched
Torrential rains did pour
The song was heard no more
And only tiny whistles from the wind
The fragile claws dug in
To crumbling shifting sand
And held a rigid steady frantic stare
As if to say the nod
Of such a small applaud
Could make a difference in the grander scheme
The music answered back
Its genuine attack
And held the count to operatic theme
With feather-laden muck
And beak accurse with straw
The tiny bird looked up
And saw the limb lie there
So crawling to its broken former perch
Waited for the sun to
Strengthen more

Matthew's Prayer

Prayer:

Help me to accept with courage the
    responsibilities
You have entrusted unto me

Matthew

Many long for you
Many have lost you
Yet God sees fit to bless me
And I'm holding you

May I not rob you of or cut short these few
    and fleeting moments of your life when you
    are totally and blissfully helpless. Even now
    as I hold you, I feel the arms of tomorrow
    tugging at you.

Yet you are so quick to trust, to love. A fresh
    new life free of worries and cares and
    responsibilities. You need me so much. I
    pray I will not fail to be there.

May I treasure you in your helplessness,
    thanking God above for sending such a
    priceless gift to me: my son.

Cup of Hope

Like a conk attached desperately to the bark—
But the cold flakes can't compare to your touch
Straighten your back—let me melt all the
    curves
Into planks of planed beauty
I am able
You are here
Art alive for the sky to breathe
Beauty above the rainbow
Warm peace

Dance Upon My Heart

Through the boroughs and the galleys
Past the sweaty din of sway
Could be heard the gritty whispers
Of the labored darkened men
Hungry yes and thirsty more
From the length of weary wage
Some were brash another saddened
But 'twas every miner's wish
To be welcomed past rememberin'
Those forgotten minutes waxed
Far away beneath the daisies
Far away below the day
And I think I may have granted
Just one hapless bit of mist
To the tall one in the corner
When his wincing frown bequest
Placed a bet without a bluff
For that icy foaming pint
And I saw his blue eyes dance
Upon my heart

Job Security

Pappa bagged an antelope
Swiftly strung it up
Momma boiled an Irish stew
Filled their empty cup

Kids can't hear the dinner bell?
Chewed that jerky through?
Clean the rifle, load some shot
Scope a deer...or two.

Communion

Ever busy, ever strong,
Sewing hope to summer's wrong.
Weaving time with threads of peace
We sing a quilted song

Proclamation

Why did God make song birds
Their music to fulfill
Just at the breaking of the dawn
When all else lies so still?
Royalty's announcement
The trumpet of the King
To herald His gift of morning
That's why messengers sing!

Truth

Jesus is the Truth!
He is the Victory!
Jesus is the Light!
The rest are history!

Consolations

Kisses from children and apple pies baking,
Candy canes, sunrises, wet puppies shaking,
Ladybugs, laughter, and rides on a swing,
These are the pleasures that pass heaven's
    door;
Give them, accept them, but treasure them
    more!

Voyage

Show me where the wind blows,
Take me there on moonbeams,
Over ocean billows
White with laughing daydreams.
Till I reach an enclave,
Secret schemes of Nature;
Then with visions God gave,
Be a heaven-seeker.

Faith

Plant a lily coming in
Adorn one going out
Into the temple of the trees
Refreshed by nature's shout
And ere the sorrows flee away
Into the branches there
Who move aside so willingly
To hear the raptor's cheer.

This Day

This day dawns to you,
There's morning in your eyes
Thoughtfulness as crisp as a rainbow
Revolves like an orange carousel
Within your soul
With cool clouds of generosity
You lift others to mountain peaks
A great gust of grace will flow forever within
    you
And be warmed by the sun of your mind, for
This day dawns to you.

The Seven Geese

I wonder should I venture
Past the meadowland today?
The tender shoots between my toes
Would not find thistles sway.
I stabbed fate at the door that day
To stroll a path unknown
Grabbed hold of crisp and preening air
Of gusts and puffs alone.
I would have missed the seven geese
Wing by on gilded song.

Comforter

With my head on His knee
He comforts me
Hiding me from the hurt
Steadfast is He.
My shelter from the cold
Forever there
Never left or alone
Warm in His care.
His voice wraps around me
Tears wiped away.
Through the storms and anguish
Here He will stay.

Glory

Soon to come
Our waiting King
Still beneath the
Buds of spring
Burst Ye forth
On clouds to bring
Ever the Hope
To Earth we sing!

The Search

How will I ever be found if I'm lost?
When will the pandering end?
Who can enlighten a wandering regret?
What if the pleadings and longings aren't met?
Will I utter the truth
To destiny's call
For all that I've woven and worn?
But if loving is missed
And sorrow is kissed
Will I ride past the dawn, past the morn?

Healing

A heart that's been broken
And chiseled by pain
Is able to love more
For tasting the rain
Flames once sweet as nectar
Grown bitter and dim
Carved a door in the heart
Now open to him

So Much More

If it were only nails and sword
Unquenched thirst and thorny crown

That pierced the Savior's side that day
That slowly drained His life away

Then death would come with pain indeed,
Death upon a Roman tree.

The pain alone He'd gladly bear
But so much more He carried there.

And yet I think this Christ can't know
What loneliness can face me.

When hatred tears a home apart
The sorrow of a broken heart.

"Reproach hath broken my heart, and I am full
  of
heaviness; and I looked for some to take pity,
  but
there was none; and for comforters, but I found
  none.,"

Yes, Jesus knew of loneliness –
Of personal rejection

For all of mankind's bravest men
Not one was there to help Him then.

Yet I wonder if a teacher
Of love and peace and goodness

Could know my vicious enemies
Of tension and anxiety?

"And being in an agony, he prayed more
    earnestly;
and his sweat was, as it were great drops of
    blood
falling down to the ground."

Christ tasted of depression's wine;
He knew of fear and sorrow.

He could have left; instead He prayed;
And now I wonder why He stayed.

Supplication

Set my feet on sacred orbit.
Blazed and cleared by angel's breath.
Firmly fix my heart to Spirit
With His crimson-hammered death.
Hone my straining ears to hear it:
"Enter in," the Father saith.

Impasse

On one point, Time and I cannot agree:
That he must keep me constant company.

Thank You, Lord

The days can be hectic, Lord, and so full of
    tasks undone. The goals I set with selfish
    thoughts become so soon the very ones
    from which I run. Today, I boast, will be a
    day. I'll build and I'll create. I'll rid the world
    of inequality, pray my neighbor out of
    iniquity and into God's perfect will.

But for mercy and grace,
For the smile on a face,
For giving me a place—
Thank you, Lord.

Trying so hard to make today live up to
    yesterday. But failures, weaknesses, and
    mistakes blur a vision I have of what my life
    could be. Losing the element you give, Lord.
    The stone on which I live all my dreams and
    tomorrows. Is there any good reason to ever
    hope again?

But for a day's work done,
For the battles I've won,
For giving me your Son—
Thank you, Lord.

I grow so tired of repetitious tasks, of meeting
    the demands, of everything I'm asked to
    do for everyone. I have my own life to live.

A busy day comes to an end, and I think I'll
rest a while; then a brother comes in need,
and I'm asked to walk another mile with his
problems and his needs. The search for me
should not be burdened with the selfish
whims of others, Lord.

But for the crown you wore,
For the cross that you bore,
For giving hope and more—
Thank you, Lord.

My eyes, so limited , see only my little world of
problems and pains. Reaching out to others
is a hard lesson to learn. When I refuse to lift
up my eyes and look beyond into Christ's, I
miss a whole new life: the one He want me
to have. Help me to begin the search within
my own heart, Lord.

But for mountains and sea
And for dying for me,
For giving love to me—
Thank you, Lord.

Savannah

Breath on a dandelion
Hope in a shadow
Hands in a circle
Savannah on a cloud

Walks in the snow
Watermelon flight
Dahlias in spring
Savannah, make me proud

Darling of the day
Beauty of the night
Precious ballad to be sung
Savannah, sing it loud!

It's a beautiful thing

When two become one
Hers is his undone
It's a beautiful thing
This love that separates the grasping
Of all we want
All we think we have to have
It's a beautiful thing
The way it all comes together
How the dreams crash through that wall
Erected by deceitful limitation
Now in all its glory
A castle in the sky
Stars blinding the naysayers
Sun shining in on this duet
With songs of triumph
Captured prey…
We laugh in victory!

Seeds

When someone cares about another
Love is planted in the soil of life.
Blooming soon or blooming late
Beauty springs forth in bursts of color.
That's the promise of harvest:
A joyful heart!

Moon Dance

No locket lies about her neck.
No ringlets fall on ivory breasts.
But silver marks the midnight trek
Of king and queen's bequests.

Lovers

Leading the pack
Through the cliffs
Through the crag

Up the steep sand
Down the banks
Toward the flag

Here come the true
With a nod
With a grin

Resolute team!
If you match
You will win!

Perpetual Style

We call out Naomi at eventide,
but Mother at break of dawn.
For all we are learning close at her side,
for rhapsodies come and gone;
I bow my head in thanks and pride
for the One who has passed this on
to all who are honored to grow beside
the face of an angel, the grace of a swan.
There's beauty that time will never hide
from Naomi at eventide.

Reception

To my dream in the forest I flee,
Where the breezes salute
And the sky wears a suit,
For the bear and the river and me.

It's Your Love...

It's your love...
That fills my heart's empty corner
With its tenderness.
It's your love...
On a dark and stormy night that
Comes in and comforts me.
It's your love...
That carries rainbows to my
Saddened weeping soul
It's your love...
From those blue eyes that lights the
Flaming fires of passion
And when the chilling winds of loneliness blow,
      you
Chase them all away with your warm and
      gentle voice.
When they blow, I have a shelter. My darling ~
It's your love.

Long-Term Forecast

Woke up on a Sunday
Taste of coffee in the sky
A coyote in the distance
But no one told me why

Is there any sense in wond'ring?
Wipe the whiskey off your chin
I heard the ravens warning
"There's a storm a rollin' in!"

How many days have wandered
Over sullen mossy stones
To smooth the Himalyas
Into silken angels' bones?

So let the thunder roll
Watch the clouds unfurl
You're bound to see a rainbow
Change this pewter into pearl.

Reunion

Today, my love, I wish for us
One day to fly above the separation
To forget a moment
Of all the burdens we carry.
A day to live only for each other.
When our minds will understand only
The screech of a gull
Or the roar of pounding waves.
To share the moon's silver reflection
And feel cold wet sand on our feet.
To savor the aroma of a hot boiling crab
On a salty breeze.
A wish to relive a thousand precious memories.
A wish to create a new one in the ecstasy of our
    love.

Portrait

Today will forever be etched in the sky
Of all of the evenings and mornings gone by
To finally end in a sunset of glory
Of purples and raisins
Emblazoned before me.
Today add a hue, Lord,
Of servant-to-King;
Brush gold into shades of a bountiful spring.
To lift up the burdened
The artist must say
Let me live with faith for today.

Mountain Man

If today I could choose where to hang my hat
When the sun slips beneath the far hill
It would not be a castle or high-rise flat
That could beckon my soul to rest still
But a wide open space where it's still not wrong
When a gent tips his hat to a gal
Far away from the clamoring stylish throng
And just east to the friendly corral.
Where I won't hear an opera tell tales off-key
Just a tune the coyotes compose
And a hard day at labor and I agree
To the bliss of a peaceful repose.
Hear the welcoming red tail announce each day
Feel the afternoon sun on patrol
See the deer and the wapiti pass this way
A prescription from God to my soul.
I'm still free to carry a bow and a gun
Smiles are plenty and arguments few
The prairie dogs labor and horses still run
Out where God made the mountains turn blue.

III – Songs

"Sing unto the Lord a new song, and His praise
from the end of the earth…"

Psalm 42:10a KJV

In the Shadow of His Hand

There are times
When all I see
Are the dark'ning clouds above me
And the fears roll in
Like waves upon the sand
Then the mighty hand of God
Covers me and I am sheltered
Safely I'm hidden
In the shadow of His hand

Chorus:
I'm in the shadow of His hand
Who shall I fear?
Who can come against me
When the mighty hand of God is near?
So through the storm
And through the fire
Bravely I'll stand
For I'm covered and sheltered
In the shadow of His hand

When I'm lost without a friend
And the road is steep before me
And I long to find some comfort for my soul
God restores my empty heart
Like a gentle breeze of mercy
He fills me up with all
I need to make me whole

Let the winter send its snow
Let the autumn leaves die sweetly
There is safety in the shadow of His hand
Though the thorns of life may pierce
Let the roses bloom with splendor
Mountains and kingdoms
Tremble at the Lord's command!
(Isaiah 49:2 & 51:15)

Who Is This Jesus?

Who is this Jesus?
Some say Moses or Elijah
Who is this carpenter of Galilee?
John the Baptist
Or a prophet
Is He just a simple fisherman
He's asking you
What will your answer be?

Chorus:
I call Him King of Kings
I call Him Lord of Lords
The Son of God
The Rose of Sharon
Emmanuel the Great I Am
Bright Morning Star!
I call Him Master, Savior
Light of the World
Wonderful, Counselor
Eternal Father, Mighty God
The Prince of Peace!

Who is this Jesus
Working miracles and wonders,
Claiming God sent Him here
To set me free?
They just mocked Him
And they cursed Him
And they crucified this Jesus

Who is this Man who says
He died for me?

Who is this Jesus?
Even death could not destroy Him
He says the time to
Trust in Him is now
While He's calling
Fall before Him
Cause He's coming back
To earth again
When that day comes
Then every knee will bow!

In the Midst of the Storm

I have this treasure in my earthen vessel
That power may be of God and not of me
My light affliction is for but a moment
And works a more eternal weight of glory

Chorus:
I may be troubled on each side yet I am not
    distressed
I'm persecuted and cast down but not forsaken
When I'm perplexed I won't despair—who can
    destroy me
When God is there in the midst of the storm?
When God is there in the midst of the storm?

(II Corinthians 4: 7–18)

Follow Me

When the darkness overtakes me
Angry storms of life engulf me
When my aimless soul's held captive
In the hurricane
There's no sorrow like this blackness
No tomorrow, only sadness
I can't hear You Lord amidst the deaf'ning pain

Bridge 1 & 2:
Don't You care that the raging waves surround
    me?
Driving hope to the fathoms of the deep
Lord, You've always been my Anchor
Through so many stormy seas
I'm still holding while the mighty oceans roar
But I just can't find the harbor anymore

Chorus:
Follow Me! Weary sailor
Follow Me! cried the Master
Lift your head; there's a lighthouse on the shore
Follow me! On the water
While the thunder billows roar
Use your faith as a compass, and I'll calm the
    raging sea
Trim the sails, set your course, and follow me!

Like a ship adrift in madness
On an unforgiving sea

Faith's the anchor that I lower
As the fury raves
But my wind-torn sails are feeble
Rocks and reefs have crushed the bow
Now I'm sinking deep beneath the pounding
    waves

When a bitter end seemed certain
Caught a vision on the foam
Felt a mighty hush of silence
Heard the waves stand still
Where the moon and stars were darkened
Sunlight kissed the salty deck
Then the Captain of the capsized cried, "Be
    still!"

Bridge 3:
Lord, You care that the raging waves surround
    me.
Driving hope to the fathoms of the deep

And You've always been my Anchor
Through so many stormy seas
Faith is guiding me to step out on the foam
Lord, I'm ready now to follow You back home

(Matthew 14:22–33)

Elisabeth

How the joy in a day
All too soon slips away
Like the sound
Of a distant chiming church bell
But the memories so deep
They're the ones that I keep
They're the ones
That I'll cherish
For a lifetime

Chorus:
Like Elisabeth, Elisabeth
Elisabeth May
Once I held her in my arms
Today I'll give her away
But I won't forget this beauty
Dressed in satin and pearls
How we looked at each other
The way she smiled
Just like her mother
Or the smell
Of white gardenias
On her wedding day

There is cheer in a smile
But for only a while
Like the wind drifting by
On clouds of laughter
Take the gifts that are rare

Like a hope and a prayer
They're the ones
To be cherished ever after

There is peace in the soul
When a heart is made whole
Like the rain finding
Sapphire in the sunshine
So most precious and dear
Are the ones I hold near
Thank you, Lord, that Your mercy
Is for all time.

Jesus, Why Did You Die for Me?

One day I hope to meet my Savior up in glory
In that place that He's preparing just for me
There I'll love to hear Him tell the old, old story
What now seems so dark I then will clearly see
I'll see how He placed the colors in a rainbow
And He'll explain how He made eagles proudly
    fly
But there yet remains a mystery still no one
    seems to know
And so I'll ask Him in the by and by:

Chorus:
Jesus, why did You die for me?
Trade Your crown for the cross of Calvary?
Why'd You leave Your home in glory
Let them nail You to a tree
Crying, "Father, why hast Thou forsaken me?"
When with just a single word from Thee
Heaven's angels would have set you free
Jesus, why did you die for me?

Unchanging Love

When the sun rises up to begin a bright new
    day
How my heart hugs those wide open skies
Then while life slips away and sunsets turn to
    gray
How I long for a love that never dies

I have dreams of my own lighting up the road
    ahead
Hurried plans, expectations, and goals
But when promises said
End up failing instead
I'm swept out in a sea of broken souls

When the silver and gold and treasure fade
    away
I learn love's something money can't buy
Then I plead and I pray
But there's nothing left to say
I'm as lost as the moon without the sky

Chorus:
V 1 & 3 –
I need an unchanging love
When the world is so uncertain
One thing that's constant and true
When the walls fall down around me
And my heart breaks in two
Who will never forsake me?

Only God up above
He's my strength
He's my comfort
He's my unchanging love

V2 –
Searching for unchanging love
When the world is so uncertain
Someone that I can count on
When the walls fall down around me
And my heart breaks in two
To come in and assure me
There's a heaven above
Like the strength and the comfort
Of God's unchanging love

(Malachi 3:6)

Alone with God

My heart's broken
Torn by the grief I feel
Words unspoken
How can they heal?
Someone listen
Hear my cries above the sunlight
Tears that glisten
Find direction through the night

Chorus:
Into a safe and quiet place
Alone with God, before His face
Into the arms of His constant embrace.
With wings so wide, He holds each care
No secrets kept
My soul laid bare
To He who pieces my spirit I cling
All that I have, He gave to me
All that I am or hope to be
I find in Jesus
My Master and King

Joy forsaken,
Darkness surrounds the day
Treasures taken
Stolen away
Sorrow, weeping
Echo through the empty shadow
Hope is sleeping
With my shattered dreams I go

Were you there then?
Can you explain to me
Secrets hidden
Deep in the sea?
There is only One
Who answers every question
Hear Him call me
To His open arms I run

(Dedicated to the families and friends of the
victims of TWA Flight 800)

There's Just No Telling

When the road is all uphill
And my heart is restless still
It is to Jesus this weary soul must go
In honest nakedness
My deepest sins confess
I cry; He listens
No truer friend I know
There's just no telling how
Jesus comforts me
A bright star in the night
Through darkness I can see
He knows how far I've roamed
His arms say, "Welcome home!"
And though I fail Him much
He heals me with His touch
There's just no telling
How Jesus comforts me
There's a castle made of trees
That He built for days like these
To lift my cares away
With a soft and gentle rain
When sorrow plagues my soul
He makes the clouds unroll
And He sends an eagle
To echo love's refrain
There's just no telling
How Jesus comforts me
A bright star in the night
Through darkness I can see

He knows how far I've roamed
His arms say, "Welcome home!"
And though I fail Him much
He heals me with His touch
There's just no telling
How Jesus comforts me

All the Tears

I'll be ready when the Savior
Comes to call me
To my home beyond the starry skies
Then I'll hear the precious voice
Of my Master
And He'll wipe all the tears from my eyes
Every sin is forgotten
No shackles of pain
Cast away all the sorrowful cries
He'll erase every heartache
And heal every wound
When He wipes all the tears from my eyes

Chorus:
All the tears from my eyes
Every wrong, every wicked compromise
Will be gone as far as
East is from the west
When He wipes all the tears from my eyes

There Is None Like You

Oh, Lord, there is none like You
So faithful so strong and true
From the rising of the sun
Until the day is done
My Lord watches over me and you
Oh, Lord, there is none like You!

Remember

When the night of my life
Comes stalking like a shroud
When so many trials surround me
Like a dark and sinking cloud
That's when a still, small voice
Deep within me seems to say
"Remember, just remember
What took place on Easter day."

Chorus:
I see the stone roll away
Then hear Jesus' voice so sweetly say
"It is I; do not fear
I have arisen my child!"
To see His face
And touch the nail prints in His hands,
O how beautiful that morning
Must have been!
O how beautiful that morning
Must have been!

Today was filled with trials and tears
I almost lost the strength to fight
All alone I struggled on
In search of just a little light
That's when a still, small voice
Deep within me seemed to say
"Remember, just remember
What took place on Easter day."

Time goes by, and life's so hurried
That sometimes I just forget
The joy I felt within my soul
When at the cross my Lord I met!
So now I want to sing, I want to shout and say
"I remember, Lord, I remember,
What you did that Easter day!"

IV – Narratives

"For by Him were all things created, that are in heaven, and that are in the earth, visible and invisible, whether they be thrones, or dominions, or principalities, or powers—all things were created by Him, and for him; And He is before all things, and by Him all things consist." Colossians 1: 15–17 KJV

At the Diner

Her cheap silver bracelet clanged on the cash
register as she mechanically rang up another
sale. Reaching slowly for the damp cloth she
had left lying on the counter behind her, the
rough-looking redhead carelessly swept the
crumbs left by her last customer on to the
cracked tile floor.

"Messy blamed people!" And she slapped the
smelly cloth back on the counter.

Reaching her hand inside her uniform spotted
with egg yolk and coffee, she pulled up a
hanging bra strap.

Her eyes darted suddenly to the old wooden
door in front of her now half ajar. Its one
hinge moaned and creaked with age and
wisdom.

The deep, scratchy voice of a large man could
be heard. "Yeah, you bet, and good luck to
you," came the voice.

The man sauntered up to the counter and, with
a wide grin, spoke to the redhead. "Mornin',
gorgeous. Beautiful day, isn't it?" The hand
he held in his pocket now pulled out a
pack of Camels. "Yeah, yeah," grumbled the

woman, tugging at her tight uniform. "Why don't ya wipe them big beautiful feet a' yers, ya' lummix? Where's yur blasted manners?"

As the large man was lighting his cigarette, he said somewhat teasingly between puffs, "Okay, all right, Louise; just calm down now. I apologize for not wipin' my feet. I just didn't want to dirty my boots on your rug! You just fix me up some ham and eggs and coffee and I'll be outa' here in less than fifteen minutes." He took a seat and fitted as best he could his long legs underneath the narrow counter.

"Watch them cracks or you won't make it past five, buster. You smart-alecky truck drivers is all the same."

The man remained calm, and he whistled as he replaced his matchbook under the cellophane of his cigarette pack.

Working with quick and careless movements, the redhead slid the man's coffee before him.

"Nope," she said without looking at him, "people just don't give a darn anymore… people gotta' care about people."

Stirring his coffee, the man looked toward the
redhead, who was tuning two greasy eggs
onto a piece of cold ham. "I'll have to agree
with ya there, Louisey baby. Take the people
in this little town for instance…why I been
drivin' truck in this state for eight years now,
and I know for a fact that none of them
gives a darn about people."

"Oh yeah," she sneered, and holding a spatula,
she placed her hands on her hips. "And just
what is it that makes you so all-fired sure a'
yerself?"

Trying to look very serious, he returned, "Well,
if they had any concern for their fellow man
at all, you'd think they'd put at least one
decent restaurant in town."

She jerked up from her work and glared at him.
Mumbling under her breath, she sloppily set
his food in front of him. Laughing, he picked
up a tarnished fork and hungrily began to
eat.

The woman watched for some time and then
began, "You know, I work like a dog to keep
this place clean, but it's a hopeless case
as long as there's people like you, thinkin'
a' nobody but yerselves. Same thing my
Joe used to say, rest his soul. Kind of glad

though he don't have to put up with it no more. A man kin just…"

"Oh stop, stop!" sobbed the man mockingly. "You're breaking my heart!"

Reaching in his wallet, he laid three dollars on the counter. "Here, Louise, my little turtle dove. Keep the change…buy yourself a handkerchief or something," he chuckled and then hesitated as if waiting for a reaction.

"Git out—out!" she snapped, storming around the counter, "or I'll carry ya out!" And she let the spatula in her hand fly, missing the man's head and hitting the door as it slammed shut.

Her cheap silver bracelet clanged on the cash register as she rang up another sale. Reaching slowly for the damp cloth she had left lying on the counter behind her, the redhead carelessly swept the crumbs left by her last customer on to the cracked tile floor.

"Messy blamed people!" And she slapped the smelly cloth back on the counter.

Seasons

I never had time to take today for the
pleasantries of life. I didn't escape to the
garden or steam away my cares in a hot
tub. The remaining yellow leaves blew like
colored rain through the quietness of the
outside sky, and I wondered how life inside
could be so different. So many tasks for
me to do. While the leaves, whose season's
work was ending, were content with
winter's onset, my life seemed trapped in a
perpetual springtime of duties…something
new to call upon my energies each day and
night.

I didn't write a song today or wile away the
hours walking through the woods. The cup
of my desire was poured out into other
empty hearts. I thirst for relief. Don't ask
me to be capable today; I don't want to be
efficient or reliable. It's time to play now,
isn't it? Like a recess from class or a new
moon, even a hibernation or a migration,
give me change! But again I go, and soon
even sleep becomes a reward, though I
know what awaits me at dawn.

No, I didn't hike or build or climb or even drive
for miles into the horizon and explore the
day today. But I have hope in my tomorrows.

Oh, God, please never take that hope! I know those days have all been planned by You. Like the first bud of spring, like crackling snow-covered grass, like the summer roses, and, yes, even like the coveted yellow leaves, I too will have a respite. You care for me just as You are asking me to care for others who are in need and to finish each task You set before me. You won't let me go unrewarded. Though I may not sit back in my chair tonight and gaze admiringly at some creation of my own or drift calmly away in relaxed ease, I will know in my heart and soul that I have obeyed You and pleased You when I offered a warm smile, a helping hand, or an encouraging word. You saw every extra load I carried, and I know You will give me a harvest of rest in time. I have stopped to thank You, to love You, to think of You, to kneel my thoughts before Your face and offer what meager gasping gift of prayer I could muster to tell You that I am content to serve You. This is the treasure that never fades away, one that remains forever, unlike portraits or buildings or gardens. Love given unselfishly will never fade away because You see each selfless, sacrificial deed no matter how small.

The Metamorphosis

We build our hopes with faith's strong arms,
  trusting and walking bravely on—our
  thoughts as eternity, not seeing an end to
  the joy that possesses our being and gives
  life to dreams.

Hopes are our escapes, so strong and yet so
  fragile. Then comes one who would dare
  to assassinate this intimate revealing of our
  hearts.

I see what was moments ago so high and
  unconquerable, like a mighty mountain,
  drug low and made to taste bitter defeat.

What passes in the night I cherish and savor
  and store in precious memories.

Yes, even what is purely strength and
  determination can suddenly find itself
  vulnerable, wrapped helplessly in arms of
  softness. Slowly and evenly, he breathes
  now and opens sleep's beckoning door.

Already his heart begins a reviving, drawing
  from her breasts that priceless treasure
  wherein all life is nourished and lives.

He will hope again as he turns her love into new and different dreams with the dawn of tomorrow to light his way.

Rejoicing!

Teach me to accept the course of each day. May
I not regret the tasks I've done or selfishly
covet those left undone.

Help me to remember that You control the
element man will never harness. You, Father,
hold the reins of time and are the master-
designer of all my days.

Paint joy and contentment within my heart just
as You have created the hours and minutes
of this day with an originality that can never
be duplicated.

Can all my dreams and hopes and plans be
satisfied by or condensed into a single day
of living?

Teach me to rejoice in the present. Grant me
the vision to see that it is the accumulation
of days spent in faith, trusting Christ to
guide me into my fullest potential and the
greatest joy that make up my lifetime.

Springtime in Our Hearts

Character and personality are intricate threads
of a life tightly woven together to form
an individual unique and separate from
all others. Yet some lives are much more
pronounced, catching and capturing first
the eye and then the heart. Like a sunbeam
filtering through twisting leaves and casting
a bright glare on a warm cheek, some
choose to stop and gaze back in curiosity
with hand-covered brow. The leaves are a
placid green and harmonize with the wind.
Others, blinded by the glare, press on and
ignore it but won't soon forget. Haven't we
all met such a life as this one, who strikes a
glow on a darkened day or adds some hope
to the smallest despairs? For this reason, you
are like springtime. To all of us here, you've
been our spring in some way. Spring is not
only a welcomed change from winter's dulls
but also offers hope and anticipation. It is
the evidence of a bountiful summer ahead!
You're soft and subtle like a spring crocus,
not brash and loud like summer dahlias.
You offer a refreshing pathway to renewal
like the buds and blossoms on awakening
trees by encouraging and motivating others.
Watching the birth of spring is how it feels
to be your friend and daughter. We are
privileged to be seven threads woven into

your life and to know that your colors and
characteristics will always be golden strands
in each of our lives. Springtime is newness,
and you are always new and fresh in all
you do. You're like a bird busily gathering
materials for a nest. And like the season,
you make the ordinary become something
extraordinary through your flavorful
attitude. What was mundane becomes
provocative just because you put in it your
pocket for a bit.

In the spring, countless blades of green
grass shoot up from thirsty soil, much
like memories from all the springs past.
Memories of feelings and pictures of sounds
and smells and flavors: Remember a fall
from a tree, a stinging, scraped knee, and
the comforting voice with the power to heal
instantly?
Remember feeling pride well up when
classmates wondered whose mom was so
pretty in the crisp blue dress, knowing she
was yours?
Remember the inviting aroma of steaming
brown pancakes and bubbling maple syrup
on an early school morning?
Remember how a Christmas present wasn't
quite "Oh, just what I wanted!" until after a
tight hug around Mom's neck?
And remember the lesson learned for a lifetime

from watching her tired eyes light up when a late husband came in weary, worn, and hungry?
It's hard to forget those cold daybreak mornings in the back of a truck, clutching quilts and each other all the way to the strawberry patch!

Memories that could fill acres and acres of dormant fields with fresh green grass. Grass that feels tender and wet and cool on bare feet. Springtime is you because of your mutual beauty. The hopeful spirit of spring will always remain to be enjoyed after every winter season, and so will our love for you.

Octagon of Trust

One should stop once and step outside the
    vicious circle of life for at least an instant
    and into a partial octagon of reality, where
    human beings are voluntarily aware of the
    never-ending arts of nature—a world where
    all inhabitants exist in martyrdom, living and
    dying for the principles of nature. All aspects
    of nature owe their great success to one
    mutual understanding called *trust.*

Since we as humans are not aspects of nature
    but rather self-decisive, self-controllable
    beings, we do not all contain this
    understanding and are not, therefore, as
    successful, beautiful, or perfect.

The thunder must trust the lightning to
Strike before it dares to roll

The sun must trust the rainbow to appear
Before it sheds light on the moist earth below

Even a squirrel must trust the oak tree to
Manifest time by its altering leaves as the great
    clock of nature slowly unwinds

And the life of a flower lies in its trust
For the dubious insect assigned

The earth must have trust in the will of God
To safely guide her through every orbit

And if Earth's plant life has no trust in
Heaven's sun rays, would not all plant creation
    lay morbid?

The stars must have trust in the nightly
Blanket of darkness to reveal and conceal them,
    to be praised and forgotten

So also does new green grass trust the rain to
    pour down food and leave it sodden

V – Youth

"Remember now thy Creator in the days of thy
youth, while the evil days come not, nor
the years draw near when thou shalt say, I
have no pleasure in them; while the sun or
the light, or the moon, or the stars, are not
darkened, nor the clouds return after the
rain; in the day when the keepers of the
house shall tremble, and the strong men
shall bow themselves, and the grinders
cease because they are few, and those that
look out of the windows are darkened, and
the doors shall be shut in the streets; when
the sound of the grinding is low, and he
shall rise up at the voice of the bird, and all
the daughters of music shall be brought
low; also when they shall be afraid of that
which is high, and fears shall be in the way,
and the almond tree shall flourish, and the
grasshopper shall be a burden, and desire
shall fail; because man goeth to his long
home, and the mourners go about the
streets; or ever the silver cord is loosed, or
the golden bowl is broken, or the pitcher is
broken at the fountain, or the wheel broken

at the cistern; then shall the dust return to the earth as it was, and the spirit shall return unto God, who gave it. Vanity of vanities, saith the Preacher; all is vanity."

Ecclesiastes 12: 1–8 KJV

The Challenge

As I strolled along the great sandy beach and
viewed all the wonders of this small portion
of a magic world pregnant with never-
ending mysteries and bursting proudly with
a glorious and superior beauty, the wild
and exotic thoughts swimming through
my curious and unsatisfied mind began
to slowly delve beneath the cotton white
caps of the rolling waves, deeper into that
familiar, distinguishing, and somehow
challenging odor of the great sea air, beyond
the wise roaring of a brave and undefeated
sea, and above the faint screeches of hungry
gulls gliding deftly through the on-looking
sky, to form a rhythmic pattern:

As I slowly strolled along the great beach
A gull yelled down a welcoming screech

The maze of waves was drawing me on
All tranquility was suddenly gone

All these thoughts probed my mind for more
    concentration
And yet a refusal by the great foaming ocean

Let there be a firmament in the midst of the
Waters, and let it divide the waters from the
    waters

As easily as that this sea was created,
A book of wonders appeared as God narrated.

"To never be known: danced the bronze
    spotted sand
Are the intricate wonders of this glorious land"

Many thoughts probed my mind for more
    concentration
Yet still a refusal by the great foaming ocean

Defeated, I turned and kissed the sea air
It replied with a playful twist of my hair

Slowly strolling along the great beach
A gull whispered down a farewell screech

11/26/68
For American Literature class

Who Are You?

When I'm rainy and cold
And feeling like the only separate thing
On earth
My heart cries out for you…
But who are you?
When will we have known together
And my soul become revived?
It is a slow death to dwell
On those whose lies were once believed
But whose love also sustained
I cannot talk to yesterday
And though I well remember
The warm hand it held outstretched
I cannot feel it
Yesterday is dead and rancid
And the hunger in my heart
Grows larger and stronger
Till I fear it may one day
Eat my soul
Dreams are tortures of tomorrow
And they devour without conscience
The soul consumes
Warm lies of yesterday
And there is pain
But preying upon its own tomorrows
Is to rot in an eternity of alone
A dream is a star
So beautiful…so deceptive!
It twinkles and glistens

And hypnotizes wholly
Begging for a touch to reach out in trust
Then snatching away each breath
Just when belief is born
Hands are cold and empty
And tomorrow laughs beautifully into eternity
Who are you? Please hear me
I have cried out for you in endless yesterdays
And tomorrow I'll die for you once again
But should we ever find together
I will give you every today my life has left

Weekends

I've always hated saying good-bye, anyway.
It hurts. *Life* is a hungry word. Then there's
tomorrow with its back turned. It wasn't
the last time I ever saw his face or heard his
voice, yet it could have been. It's the not
knowing. The flashing blur of his face as he
winded past my car on his Honda…and that
wide smile that I know so well. That was
the last picture my mind saw of Mike that
day. So full of youthfulness and love is my
brother.

"Got an extra buck, Val?"
"I loaned you two last week."
"Yeah, but I wanna' go to to the game. We're
    playing Cascade."
"What's good to eat, sis?"
"Well, I could make some potato soup."
"How 'bout some pancakes? There's already
    batter in the fridge."

"Mike, that shirt doesn't go with those pants!"
"I don't care. I'm only going to church."
"Go put a tie on."
"I don't have one."

"Where's the keys to the Mustang?"
"I'll start it up for you."
"You just stay out of it!"
"Never mind, I found them."

"Hey…I took a bath!"
"Here, comb your hair."

"When ya' comin' back, sis?"
"I'll see ya' in a couple weeks, I guess."
"Take it easy."
"Yeah, okay!"

Velvet Palette

Soft buds and blossoms
Are slowly appearing
New hungry sprouts sing
And shout, "Spring is nearing!"

The drab hazy scrimping
Of winter is gone
In the dark, spring is stalking,
Preparing to spawn

Motionless insects begin
To unveil
Singing winged creatures
Through ecstasy sail

Honey-colored meadows
Look so inviting
Bushes sway gently
And smell so exciting

Cotton-pearl clouds are
Swelling with joy
Drifting in azure
Adorning, yet coy

And the velvet portrait
Now can be framed
As the timeless work
That nature has claimed

Never

Never: such a gloomy word.
Full of nothingness yet always heard.
Brimming with emptiness and displays of not
    ever;
Stinging the silent flight of a bird.

Dusk

Clouds sink down around yawning trees.
Leaves dance wildly to the beat of the breeze.

Red blanket sunset covers the hills
As swallowing darkness strikes and kills.

Fragile

People are such
Selfish creatures
Can't they see
Their empty loneliness?
Can a soul exist
By itself?
A man is a shell
Filled with oneness
Tossed about
In an unsympathetic
Sea of progress
Nurtured only
By his own longings
Trapped in a deafening
Silence of voices
Unable to hear
His own name
How long can
Empty shells exist?

Daydrop

A day is a drop of life
Each drop is a single experience

Days can be slow and lonely
In their obstinate oneness

It is the love of friends
That consoles the torturing slowness

May a speck of gold enter
Today's drop of life for you

A Touch

Where are you?
How are you…really?
What do you feel
Inside yourself?
Do others drift by
Like a flowing breeze?
I care.

Now

Now is like a yellow meadow
Weeping early rain without a
Smile or a vibration midst
The ongoing air…

My One Valentine
Saigon
February 14, 1970

My dearest darling, my one valentine,
If I had one wish, I'd wish you were mine.

Our love was true as the stars in the sky;
I can still feel your tears as we said good-bye.

I remember last fall and the love we shared
then
But I know, my love, I'll never see you again.

I was wounded last night on the enemy line.
I can feel death approaching, my one valentine.

As I lay in this bunk and my breaths are so few,
I imagine it's May and I'm home holding you.

I've done lots of dreaming, spent each night
feeling blue,
I've relieved each kiss, every moment with you.

I can still see those blue eyes, your hair golden
and fine,
When a year ago today you said you'd be mine.

I didn't know then what was lying ahead.
Though this day is my last, our love is not dead.

God made me a promise, and it's helped me
    face death,
That one day we'll meet on a white cloud of
    breath.

But until we meet on that day so divine,
You're still my darling, my one Valentine.

In the Beginning

Man was created a sinless pure creature,
Free of all woe, truth his main feature.

Laid on his white hand an offer to be,
God's vow of peacefulness, humble and free!

"Take me, oh Lord. Caress me with chastity!"
Nay, man is fickle for he set his own destiny.

Appearance of evil; unveiling of guile.
Before him lurks Satan, fomenter of rile.

Attempt this proposal of sly condensed crime?
Oh woe! Satan purloined man's Eden sublime.

The forsaken Creator, now stabbed by
    ingratitude,
Smote man from the Garden with heavenly
    magnitude.

Man's now-blushing face abandons all
    innocence,
Scarred deep with sin, forever unworthy hence.

Rests on his gray palm great toiling and efforts,
Peace now not feasible; destruction retorts…

Since: man is militant, evil, and greedy
As man vs. man, their results come more
    speedily.

What's become of the Garden, you may never
	know,
As man lives for man to reap not to sow.

Ceremonies

Leaving behind bits
Of mud on the clean waxed floor
I ran out quickly
~~~~~~~~~~~~~~~~~~~~~~
The soft yellow down
Of a newly born chicken
Feels moist in my hand
~~~~~~~~~~~~~~~~~~~~~~
Lone quiet table
A red-stained cigarette butt
Floating in a cup

Is This Really Christmas?

It was Christmas Eve night, and the presents
  were ready.
The tree was all strung with bells and confetti.

The children were laughing and impatiently
  waiting
For Dad to say, "Go," but Dad was debating.

"Is this really Christmas?" I knew he was saying.
"Or just a big party for games and for playing?"

"It's losing its meaning," again he repeated.
"But is it their fault how their minds have been
  cheated?"

He slowly stood up and walked toward the
  chair
And picked up the Bible he found lying there.

With a puzzling silence the whole room was
  filled
As Dad turned the pages and around him we
  milled.

In Luke chapter two was the story he read,
As the little ones listened—even Robert and
  Ed!

"And suddenly there came with the angel a
    multitude
of the heavenly host praising God, and saying,
    Glory to
God in the highest, and on earth peace, good
    will toward men."

And after he read, things were better; we sang!
The Christmas tree shook, and the piano, it
    rang!

"This is true Christmas spirit!" I could see in
    Dad's smile
He was thoroughly satisfied or at least for a
    while.